Why I Love You Grandma

The Book I Wrote About Us

The Life Graduate Publishing Group

No part of this book may be scanned, reproduced or distributed in any printed or electronic form without the prior permission of the author or publisher.
Copyright - The Life Graduate Publishing Group 2021 - All Rights Reserved

⭐⭐⭐⭐⭐

We love to receive reviews from our customers. If you had the opportunity to provide a review we would greatly appreciate it. Thank you!

Send us an email if you would like to be notified of new books we release via **info@thelifegraduate.com**

Dear Grandma

Love............................

THIS BOOK IS WRITTEN FROM MY HEART. I CREATED IT FOR YOU BECAUSE.....

_____

_____

_____

_____

_____

_____

_____

_____

WHEN WE ARE APART GRANDMA, I REALLY MISS...

_____

_____

_____

_____

_____

I LOVE HEARING STORIES ABOUT...

_____
_____
_____
_____

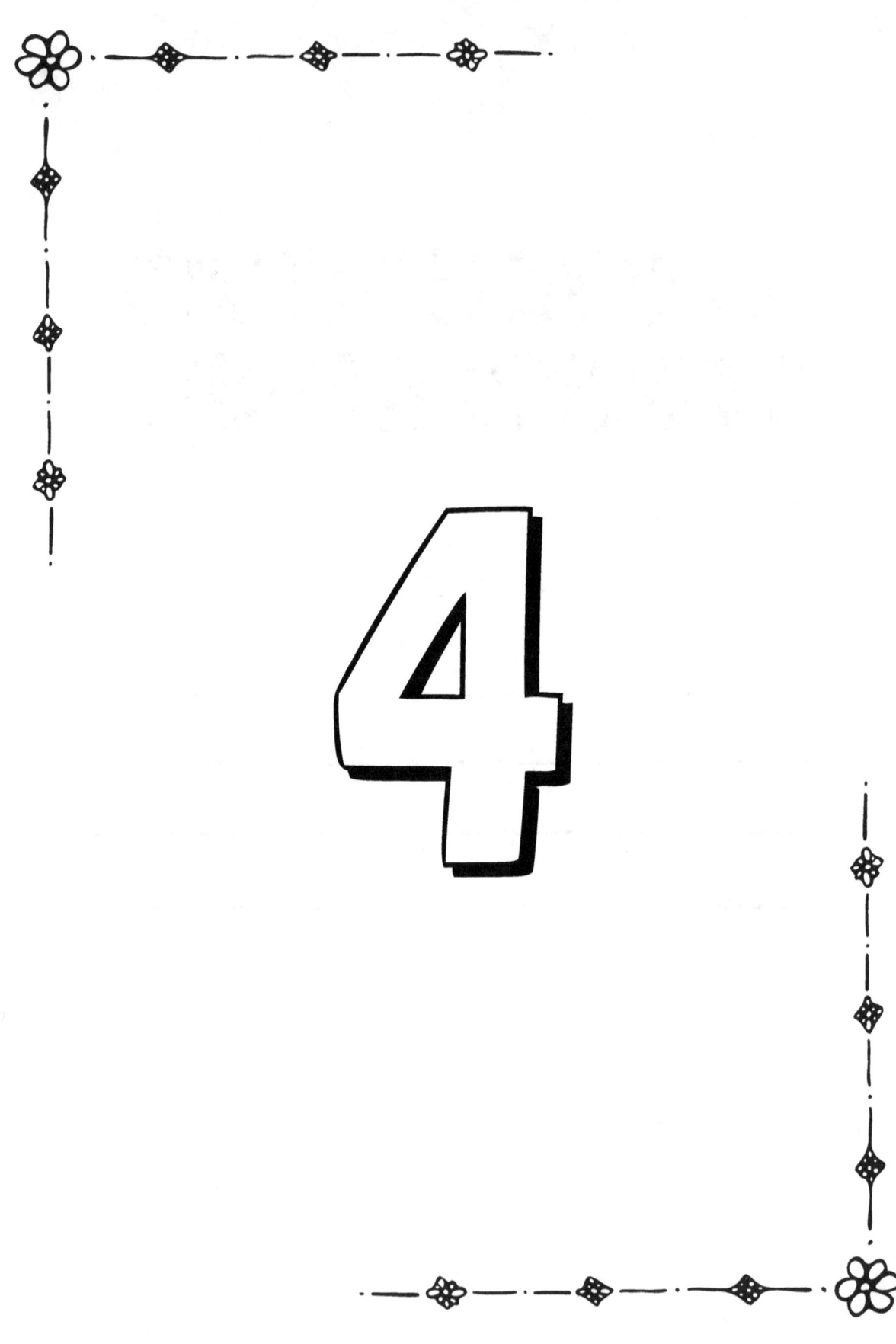

THESE ARE 3 THINGS YOU DO GRANDMA THAT ARE KIND AND THOUGHTFUL

1. _____

_____

2. _____

_____

3. _____

_____

IF I CLOSE MY EYES AND THINK OF SOMETHING SPECIAL WE HAVE DONE TOGETHER, I THINK OF...

_____

_____

_____

_____

_____

I WOULD LOVE TO CREATE A...

FOR YOU

GRANDMA, I WOULD LIKE TO SAY THANK YOU FOR....

_____

_____

_____

_____

Thank You

I'VE NEVER SAID THIS TO YOU BEFORE, BUT I LOVE IT WHEN YOU...

_____
_____
_____

BECAUSE...

_____
_____
_____
_____
_____

GRANDMA, I REMEMBER THE TIME WE....

A photo of us!

YOU MAKE ME LAUGH WHEN....

YOU MAKE ME SAD WHEN....

YOU MAKE ME SMILE WHEN....

IF I COULD TAKE YOU ANYWHERE IN THE WORLD, WE WOULD VISIT..

GRANDMA'S BOARDING PASS SEAT: **1A**

DEPARTING LOCATION

ARRIVING LOCATION

WE WOULD VISIT THIS LOCATION BECAUSE

_____

_____

_____

THIS WAS SOMETHING SPECIAL THAT YOU DID FOR ME THAT I WILL NEVER FORGET.....

_____

_____

_____

_____

_____

_____

THIS IS SOMETHING SPECIAL THAT YOU SAID TO ME...

YOU CAN DO THIS BETTER THAN ANYONE ELSE!

WHEN I HEAR YOUR VOICE, IT MAKES ME FEEL

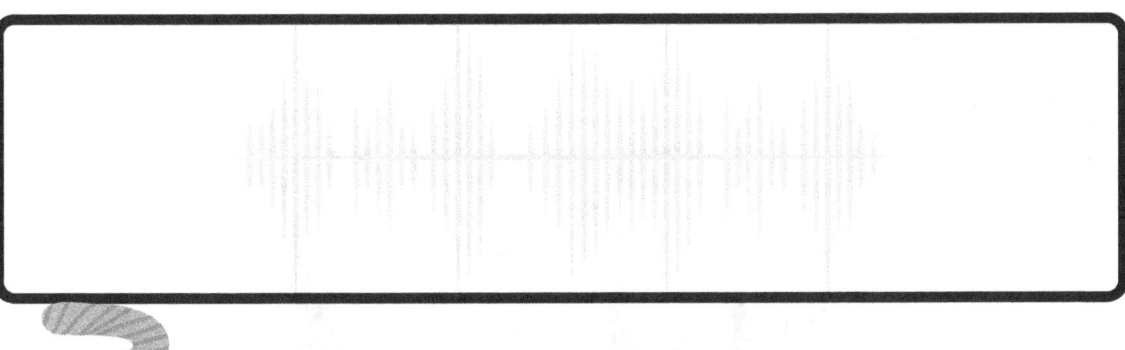

 **BECAUSE....**

17

IF I COULD MAKE ONE WISH, I WOULD WISH THAT WE...

GRANDMA, I THINK YOUR SPECIAL 'SUPER-POWER' IS.....

YOU DIDN'T KNOW THIS BUT I...

THESE ARE 3 WORDS THAT BEST DESCRIBE YOU.

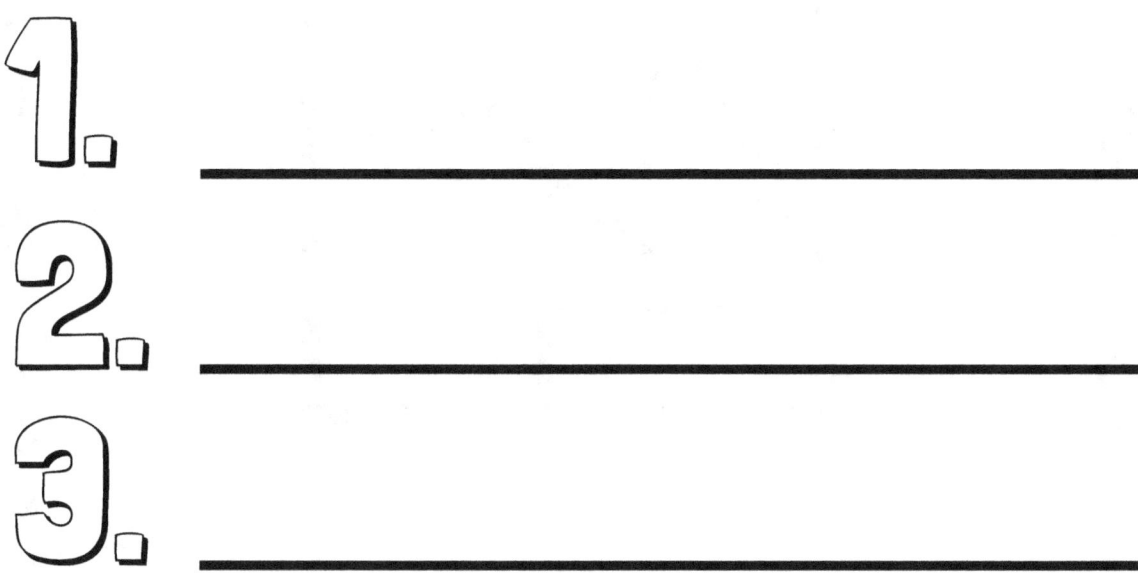

1. _____
2. _____
3. _____

GRANDMA, EVERYONE SHOULD BE AS...

_____

AS YOU!

 **This is a drawing of us**
_____

SPECIAL MOMENTS or MEMORIES

Add other special photo's or details here

SPECIAL MOMENTS or MEMORIES

Add other special photo's or details here

I wrote this book about us Grandma.

Kisses and Hugs

xoxo

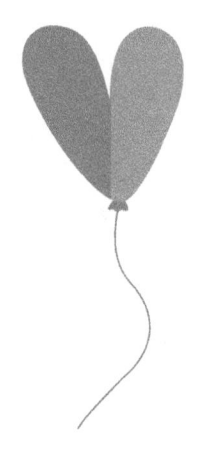

A sample of other books created by
The Life Graduate Publishing Group

www.thelifegraduate.com/bookstore

www.ingramcontent.com/pod-product-compliance
Lightning Source LLC
LaVergne TN
LVHW060145080526
838202LV00049B/4088